I0138334

By Abraham Great
Copyright ©2013 Revised 2020
ISBN: 978-1-908040-28-2

Published in the UK by:
Golden Pen Publishing Ltd

All right reserved

No portion of this book may be used without the written
permission of the publisher.
For further information or permission, contact:

Golden Pen (Publishing)
A Division of Golden Pen LTD
Milton Keynes,
United Kingdom

info@goldenpenpublishing.com
www.goldenpenpublishing.com

Cover design by Media Expression Intl (Check this)
Printed in the UK

DEDICATION

I have been a committed lover of the word of God from the age of 16. Just by reading the bible, I have found courage, strength, wisdom, understanding, power, joy, blessing, and family . However, the one thing I know the Bible continues to help me make is decisions. So, I would like to dedicate this book to the WORD.

APPRECIATION

I moved into top gear in obedience to God's word and my mentors' instructions since 2004. This feat I owe to one person: my wife, Queen Great. Not only have you been a great companion in making right decisions, you have also been meek enough to make a right turn after realizing every wrong decision made. For the motivation to write this book while raising wonderful children - a great inspiration to us both - with me, I say thank you!

To my son, Abraham Darren Great, to you I owe the title of this book and the inspiration to write it. Thank you for the listening ears during those telephone conversations in the car, which eventually culminated into the idea behind this book. A leader you are, and that you will always be. To Dexter and Divine, thank you for being on your wisest behaviours each time daddy is busy teaching or writing. You guys are Great.

This book would not have been available for print without the help of volunteers at Gr8terworks, Bola Adebola, Maxwell, Eniola Olajide, Victorial Agunbiade and Ketochi Ekpo. You guys are a great blessing and joy.

To my Big Bro, Gbenga Oladokun, A.K.A Concept, you have consistently delivered amazing results despite the deadlines and hard work your daily routine requires, thank you ever so much.

To all HLBC members, I thank you for the privilege of serving as your leader, teaching these principles that work. Indeed, it is working.

Finally, to my editor, Olusegun Iseilaiye, your ability to interpret my intentions is incredible. Thank you for your help, inspiration and patience through this project. You are destined for the top. To Dr. Boye Oloritun, thank you for spending several hours to proof read this work. You are blessed in many ways.

INTRODUCTION

Have you ever wondered how come you were born into the family to which you belong and not another? What if your parents never came together at the time they did, or they never even met at all, whose child would you have been? This imaginary question does not leave you out even if you were born out of wedlock. Perhaps you were conceived without intention via an unguarded encounter, the truth is that the decision to keep you till birth was still a matter of choice by your mother. Although your coming into being was not your decision, how you would turn out in life is up to you to decide.

My mentor and role model Dr. David Oyedepo once said, *"Life is a product of personal adventure."* Timeless truth, I reckon. O yes, we live our lives in the adventure of the choices and decisions we make daily.

Decision making is something every living being does several times on a daily basis, even when we don't acknowledge it; for lack of decision is in itself, a decision in the passive sense. Decision making an innate ability that grows with every living creature over time. Even the ant, as small as it appears, makes several decisions every day - either to move from one destination to the others or to execute some other tasks.

Decisions determine our destination in life. A single decision or a combination of them - if made wrongly - can shatter God's plan for your life. A typical example is Samson, a vessel singled out to fulfil divine agenda, gifted with unusual strength, but made foolish decisions that eventually ruined his life. You see, the fact that you are destined for greatness does not mean that you will end up great. It is still subject to the decisions you make.

One of my favorite Bible stories is that of Joseph. At the onset of his journey to greatness, his decision to amplify his dreams got him in serious troubles. This was followed by his father's decision to send him to his brothers who put him in a precarious position. His brothers unanimously decided to sell him off to the Ishmaelites who had decided to ply the road where paths would cross for that transaction to take place on that day. Buying him to be a servant was Potiphar's act of decision making. By choice, Joseph feared God. He refused lay down his chastity at the feet of seduction when Potiphar's wife stepped in to tempt him- by decision. The prison warden's decision repositioned Joseph as head of other prisoners. His decision to give expression to his gift of revelation and wise counsel prompted Pharaoh to make him prime minister. Isn't it proper to deduce here that our lives are a product of interplay and cumulation of decisions, both ours and that of those connected to us - both by choice and by circumstance? However, the onus is on us to let our own decisions lead the course of the sequence of events, so we do not blame our failure on others, for you are solely responsible for the outcome of your life. Therefore, when next someone's decision presents you lemon, decide to turn it to lemonade in your favour.

Your decisions do not only affect you; they may impact upon future generations. The occurrence that followed Joseph's enthronement was a launching pad for a cycle of decisions that became the back story preceding the Exodus: Famine struck. Joseph's family decided to travel to Egypt to find food. Then Joseph met his brothers again, forgave them; and there was a family reunion. Pharaoh decided to give the land of Goshen to Joseph's family. And there they were for over four hundred years. Another sequence of decisions!

Joseph's story rings a bell of reference till date. And if I was called upon to give the movie a screen title, I would gladly call it DECISIONS...

Your tomorrow is simply the final outcome of whatever you decide today. You are a product of yesterday's decisions. This is why I have put these thoughts together - to help you make decisions that will better your future. This book should serve as a devotional to you and your loved ones. Let all your children who are able to read join you in using this resource.

Decisions decide your life!

31

DECISIONS THAT MAKE A PERSON OF VALUE

Life begins with decisions

Abraham Great

CONTENT

DECISION TO TRUST IN GOD

1.DECISION TO TRUST IN GOD

"So that your trust may be in the LORD, I teach you today, even you." - Proverbs 22:19

That this comes first in this book is no coincidence. God is first and must be put in His place. Truthfully, the decision to trust in God is the ultimate to make in life. No other decision is more important. Unfortunately, it is overlooked by many. For some of us, God is only a back-up plan, a last resort only when all else has failed.

It is important to know some of the reasons the decision to trust in God is so crucial. They include the following:

➤ Trust in God is the foundation.

No house can stand long and strong without a solid foundation underneath. Our lives need a solid foundation. We do not live in a trouble-free world. Trouble started from the fall of man in the garden of Eden, it will not suddenly cease because of you. Sometimes, we have to deal with storms; other times, we even deal with hurricanes. To get by in the midst of them all and coming out victorious is in the hands of The Almighty.

Trust in God creates that solid foundation your life requires. It gives you the strength to wither the fiercest of storms. The Bible in *Psalm 34:19* (Amp) says *"Many evils confront the [consistently] righteous, but the Lord delivers him out of them all."* You only get delivered by a God that you stick to, just like you can only draw from a fountain you are connected to.

➤ Trust in God brings peace.

The control of the future is not in your power. Though you can plan and work hard for it, it is still subject to uncertainties. Making a decision to trust in God does not necessarily reveal to you the future, but it does place your future in His hands. If you can trust God, then you can stop worrying about the future. You can rest assured that come what may, everything will work out right. The scripture makes us understand that it has not yet been conceived by any mortal, what God has in plan for those who love Him. Furthermore, we are made know to know that His plan is that of a great future and hope. These are assurances to bank, if truly we love Him. And if we love Him indeed, we show it by trusting Him. Therefore, trust in the Lord and live in peace.

> ➤ Trust in God helps you let go of your past.

Sometimes, we make mistakes which can be the cause of ache in our souls for long years of our lives. No one can bring the time back and fix those mistakes, but God can redeem them. He has paid the price already. He has the power to forgive you and help you forgive yourself. With His love, He can help you make up for the consequences of your past iniquities and give you a new lease of life.

> ➤ Trust in God makes you a winner in the present.

Everything happens within the space of time, and God Himself is the author time- past, present and future. Therefore, at no time has anything happened without His knowledge, including the happenings in your life. If you make a decision to trust in this all-knowing God in the present, He will uphold you with the strength to make it through.

"God always gives His best to those who leave the choice with him."

Jim Elliot

"Never be afraid to trust an unknown future to a known God."

Corrie Ten Boom

DECISION NOT TO FEAR

2. DECISION NOT TO FEAR

"But whoever listens to me will live in safety and be at ease, without fear of harm." - Proverbs 1:33

Fear is a very potent emotion. Fear is actually faith in the negative. It is a very active sensation. It holds your entire being to ransom - spirit, soul and body. You are willing to move, but held down by unseen shackles- that is fear! Living in fear can be very tormenting. You may want to discover how fear works and what can be done to overcome it below.

Fear launches a flight or fight reaction in our bodies. When we are afraid, our bodies produce adrenaline. Then we are either pushed to run or paralyzed from moving. I hope you agree that neither making hasty decisions nor staying inactive is a good problem-solving approach. Whenever you make hasty decisions, you have skipped steps that lead to logical action. You have not organized your thoughts or analyzed the situation. When you fail to do these, you lose sight of possible consequences, thereby putting yourself in harm's way. On the other, if you refuse to act due to fear-induced paralysis, you can miss out on great chances in life.

So, how do you make a decision not to fear?

➤ Confront your fears

It's impossible for us to just "stop fearing". Fear is not a reaction you can just turn off. But you need to face your fears head-on. Sometimes, we are afraid of the fear itself. Sounds strange right? But look at it this way: You need to cross to a green pasture, but you have a giant before you. He has the might of Goliath, but you on the other hand lack the courage of David. Now there is a cave you can hide in which the giant cannot get into. If you seek refuge in the cave, you are protected, but only for a while because the giant is not leaving and there is no food in the cave to sustain you. The pasture is your goal, and the giant is FEAR. People refuse to face fear head-on when they are afraid it is mightier than they can handle. But if you must be victorious in life, you must face it with courage just like David did Goliath. You do not just keep saying "What if this... what if that" while sitting idly by. It is only a matter of time before you start to run out of whatever has been sustaining you while idle. The cave is not your place; come out of your shell. There is a greener pasture on the other side of life. But for you to reach it, you must make conquer that giant called fear. Greater is He that is in you. You are more capable than you think. You have underestimated your-self for far too long.

For a start, I urge you to write down all the "What If?" questions. Then try to imagine the very worst outcome for each of the situations you are faced with.

In some cases, you discover that your fear has made things look worse than they are in reality. You'd discover that you were afraid of fear itself. In other situations, knowing the worst greatly lessens your fears.

> Learn to control your body

The body and soul are closely connected. If you can stop the fear reaction in your body, you can master your soul, too. Start with breathing. Fear naturally makes you breathe fast. So first, you need to hold your breath. Learn the slow and deep breathing techniques. Fear strains your muscles. Learn to relax them. When you do this, you are gradually stabi-lizing your emotion till you gain enough balance to move on.

> Neutralize fear with faith

Fear is the opposite of faith. Actually, fear is faith, but a negative form of it as stated in the earlier. While faith is believing you will succeed, fear is believing you will fail. So, you see, fear is faith in the wrong things. Faith is the only antidote that works best for the poison of fear. Fear moves you to rush decisions, while faith enables you to wait for the right time. Fear keeps you inactive, while faith motivates you to make a step forward.

> "Expose yourself to your deepest fear; after that, fear has no power, and the fear of freedom shrinks and vanishes. You are free."

Jim Morrison

> "Faith activates God - Fear activates the Enemy."

Joel Osteen

DECISION REGARDING YOUR NEIGHBOR

3. DECISION REGARDING YOUR NEIGHBOR

"Let love and faithfulness never leave you; bind them around your neck, write them on the tablet of your heart." - Proverbs 3:3

Being social beings, we humans cannot afford to live in isolation. Realistically, fellow human beings, especially our loved ones are the biggest treasures in our lives. Thus, whatever decision we make regarding people around us is very important. What are some of those decisions that truly count? Let's take a look.

BE ON TIME

One of the key decisions you can make regarding the people around you is the decision to be on time. This does not mean keeping to time when attending events or visiting places with your loved ones (which is not a bad thing). What it really means is that you be there for people when most needed. It means coming through for them without fail when they need your affection; support- moral, financial or any other; encouragement and many more acts of love that can be thought of. Some of these gestures can be a once-in-life-time chance to really show how much we value the relationship. When we fail to be on time with it, it brings on us a lifetime regret.

You should have timely value for your dear ones. Nobody lives twice; treasure them while they are around or when they need it the most. Sometimes, we get too busy to express our love when it most matters to our loved ones. At other times, we may feel intimidated or shy to say or do something to express the love and affection for people around us.

If we have been able to hurt people in our lives sometimes with feeling intimidated or shy, why then should we get like that when it is time to show love?

BE PROACTIVE

Do not wait for people to make the first move so you can return the favour. While it is nice to reciprocate love when shown to you, you do not have to wait for them to show you first. Instead, the initiative. Be proactive, and show them love first.

FORGIVE

Another key decision to make is to forgive. Make it a rule for yourself to be the first to always forgive. Do not wait for the people you love to come and ask for forgiveness. Be generous in forgiving others, as "love covers many sins". View those offenses as trifles compared to the great gift of love and companionship.

"If you judge people, you have no time to love them."

Mother Teresa

"Not all of us can do great things. But we can do small things with great love."

Mother Teresa

DECISION TO BE A TITHER

4. DECISION TO BE A TITHER

"Honor the LORD with your wealth, with the firstfruits of all your crops; then your barns will be filled to overflowing, and your vats will brim over with new wine." - Proverbs 3:9-10

This aspect of Christianity often evokes many discussions among people with various opinions - both believers and non-believers. It has aroused so much controversies in recent times with thought leaders both for and against the practice. Nevertheless, the blessings attached to it remain sacrosanct. Now, let us take a look at some of the reasons you need to decide to be a tither.

GIVING IS NATURAL

All the relationships of humans with God have become possible only because God gave His only Son. We are to follow His footprints. This means that giving should be natural for Christians, as it is natural for God.

We must also note that no healthy relationship can be sustained without giving. Giving can be of any sort, depending on what the relationship requires to flourish. In the case of ours with God, material giving has always a been a part and parcel. It started with Cain and Abel, it continued till the days of Abraham who first gave a tithe to Melchizedek the High Priest. Jesus is our own High Priest after the order of Melchizedek. And since Abraham gave tithe to Melchizedek, then we also have a duty as Abraham's seed to pay it as we also have a high priest after the same order - Jesus Christ.

GIVING IS EXPRESSIVE

How can you judge someone's attitude towards you? How can you tell the difference between love and indifference?

You do that by judging how much a person is willing to give. Love is all about giving. "For God so loved the world that He gave..." While you may give without loving, it is impossible to love and not give. Giving is the ultimate expression of love. Therefore, tithing expresses our true attitude to God. We show our love for Him if we give and give gladly and willingly.

GIVING IS BENEFICIAL

You know why Dead Sea got that name? It's simply because there are many streams that flow into it, but none flows out. Nothing can live in the Dead Sea, because it is too salty. It takes in the water and minerals in it, then the water evaporates, but the minerals stay. That is what makes the sea salty and dead.

The same is true of a believer, who only takes in the God's blessings, but gives nothing in return. You may reach the point where you get too much and things get too dense. Life dies at that point, because there is no outflow of it. So, giving is beneficial, because it makes the room in your life for receiving fresh blessings from God.

GIVING IS RIGHT

God is the source of all your supplies. He has given you all: your life, the world around you, resources and money. It is appropriate to honour Him by giving the tithe. See, giving works the best if you have a choice of giving 10 percent away or saving it. When you give, you sow, meaning you are honouring God and He will honour you in return. When you save, you get just that 10 percent in your pocket and no prospects whatsoever for it to grow.

"Life is never tight for a tither."

Abraham Great

"Giving to God is a grace - but not giving to God is a disgrace."

Brian Kluth

DECISION TO CHOOSE

5. DECISION TO CHOOSE

"...then choose for yourselves this day whom you will serve." - Joshua 24:15

O nce you get the feeling that you are merely flowing in the streams of life, it is time to make some decisions. A most crucial one at this point is the decision to exercise your freedom of choice. It is the accurate response to the feeling of having no power over the situations in your life. Do not just subject your life to chances. You need be in charge of your own life. Decide what you want and what to do away with. You won't believe how much change you can effect in your life when you start to make your own decisions and navigate your course through life rather than just drifting through it.

How do you go about choosing? Well, the key secret of learning to choose is creating your habits. You just have to change your orientation if you have been underestimating the power of habit. There are two kinds of habit: good habit and bad habit. It is usually more challenging to form a good habit than it is to form good ones, reason being that the good ones are mostly deliberate, requiring conscious efforts, while the bad ones are manifestations of fleshly desires. Sometimes we do not even notice the negative habits we form. That is one reason decision making may be such a challenge for you.

Knowing that decision making is also a habit you can form, here is how you practically do it: Start with something small and simple. Keep in mind that forming habits takes time. You cannot revolutionize your life overnight. You have to take it bit by bit and be consistent with it. What becomes big in our lives are an accumulation of things acquired in bits over time. If you want to broaden your knowledge and sharpen your intellect for example, you know one of the best ways to achieve it is to be an avid reader. When you get on this journey initially, you do not have to finish a five-hundred-page book in twenty-four hours. You can start by reading a page, two pages or a chapter a day. Before you know it, you are swimming in a sea of knowledge and wisdom as a result of page-by-page accumulation. Forming good habits bears timeless fruits, as these habits remain there for the most part of your life.

So, pick a small habit you wish to form. Speaking of choosing, make a habit of taking a halt three times a day to think over what you are doing just here and now. Then say out loud to yourself, "I am doing this and this and I have CHOSEN to do it". It does not really matter what you find yourself doing. Just say it out loud. You may be reading a book, praying, watching TV, eating dinner late at night, etc.

You see, most of us tend to say something like this: oh, it just happened. These words indicate to us that we are mostly just drifting through life. Things happen, you know. The key thought is that you have to train yourself to admit that all these happenings in your life are possible because of your CHOICE. I have chosen not to eat late at night, I have chosen to pray, I have chosen to watch TV for three hours, etc. This exercise would show you how much power you have over choosing things and the ways to change your life for better. You train yourself to take up the responsibility for your own life.

"Action expresses priorities".

Gandhi

"The measure of choosing well, is, whether a man likes and finds good in what he has chosen."

Charles Lamb

DECISION ON WHO TO IGNORE

6. DECISION ON WHO TO IGNORE

"Wisdom will save you from the ways of wicked men." - Proverbs 2:12

The saying goes: it takes all kinds of people to make the world. However, there are some people that should not be tolerated in your life if you wish to succeed. This can be a challenge sometimes, especially when these people happen to be our colleagues, friends, superiors or people in authority who make decisions that affect us. Hence, we feel the need for their acceptance and endorsement. Acceptance is in itself not a bad thing, the problem is how we sometimes go about it. Oftentimes, we conform to wrong morals because they seem generally accepted. Due to bandwagon effects, peer pressure and other negative social factors, we get desperate not to be the odd one out. We do not want to be treated like an outcast, so in desperation for acceptance, we conform to crowd mentality. The good news is that there is a remedy for this, only if you are genuinely seeking it. Please read along as I walk you through the way out.

SET YOUR STANDARDS

This is not with intentions to people, no! Rather it is to guard you against those who can drag you down or teach you evil ways. You know, righteousness and evil are both contagious. This is why the Bible makes known to us that evil company corrupts good seed; and also, he that walks with the wise shall be wise. As a child of God, the Bible should be your standard. It is your ultimate guide to living right. David knowing this confessed thus, *"Your word is a lamp for my feet, a light to my path" (Psalm 119:105)*. God's word makes you wise to tread with caution. With it, you will gain the wisdom to discern in who to allow into your life.

Here is a simple wisdom example. You may have had problems with alcohol in your life, but got free from the addiction. In this case, making friends with people who drink much or love fun and alcohol parties may not be such a good idea. You have to be wise and count your chances - which is more likely, you pulling them out of their addiction or them bringing you down into it? Do not be deceived; it is easier for one to move down a slope than to move up. In the same vein, it is easier for them to draw you back into your addiction than for you to pull them up to freedom.

SURROUND YOURSELF WITH LIKEMINDS

Having set standards for yourself, this is what should follow. Connect and keep a company of positive people. Let them constitute your inner circle. When you keep positive people close, they will surely rub off on you. Under the influence of their exemplary conduct and positive communication, you will be motivated to keep up with the standard you have set for yourself. Remember that iron sharpens iron. This also means that while these people encourage you to be better, you too would be an inspiration to others in your circle to be better. So you see; a relationship with like-minds is symbiotic.

Once you decide which people to ignore in your life, you have made an unpopular decision. You may receive backlashes for it. But keep in mind that it is your life and you are responsible for it. You have the right to block some people out of it. Once you make the decision, stick with it. Be polite and loving, but firm in your decision to ignore those people.

"Be slow in choosing a friend, slower in changing."

Benjamin Franklin

DECISION ON WHAT TO IGNORE

7. DECISION ON WHAT TO IGNORE

"Discretion will protect you, and understanding will guard you". - Proverbs 2:11

To really effect significant improvement in the affairs of your life, one of the most important things to do is re-think your priorities and set them right. You may have heard tons of things about prioritizing. However, there are just two key things to mention here. First of all, you need to discover your real priorities and secondly, you need to keep away the distractions.

DISCOVERING YOUR TRUE PRIORITIES

A number of times you may have written a list of items you desire or wish to shop for. You are even more likely to list them in a descending order of importance to you. It is okay to regard this as a sort of priority list. However, if they are not crucial to your survival or they are not things that would help you attain your life goals, then they are not priorities. They are just items of a wish list. There is a significant difference between wants and needs. Your needs are priorities because you cannot do without them if you must survive or achieve certain things, while your wants are things that you only fancy but can do without. When in high school we were being taught in Economics the difference between wants and needs, many of us if not all, had no idea how much of a lifelong rele-vance the lesson would have. It is up to you to differentiate your wants from your needs. If you have a sum of money at your disposal, and you are to choose between buying pair of suits or putting for a leadership training which is crucial to your career advancement. Now, monetarily, these two go for the same amount of money; it does not mean they hold the same value. One holds a transient value, while the other is perpetual in its effect. Decide the value each holds in order to decide which to forgo for the other. Just bear in my that one is a mere spend which is to be ignored, while the other is an investment.

Please note that wants are not really bad. The point is that when you find your wants contending with your needs, you should ignore the wants in favour of needs.

Setting of priorities does not only apply to money and material things, it also applies to time. Just like money, time also is either spent or invested. As a matter of fact, time is far is even more important as it is irrecoverable once it passes. Therefore, prioritize your activities to determine how to use your time. Decide which activities are on of prime importance to you. For example, if that your family is of prime importance to you, juxtapose this with the way you spend your time. Are you spending your every evening and weekend with your friends at the bar rather than being home bonding with your wife and kids? Do you really spend a good portion of your time with your family? As a youth, do you spend long hours of the browsing through social media mongering gossips when you should pray and prepare for the day's task? Worthy of note is the fact that the amount of time you spend on activities you prioritize is not as important as how effectively you engage in those activities. In other words, quality of time is more important than duration. When you spend time with family, what do you actually do? A man can spend four hours of family time pointing out the faults of every other member without correcting them in love, arguing with his spouse without resolution. Another man can spend just an hour with his family, engaging them fruitfully by listening to each member's challenges and providing encouragement while reasoning out solutions with them. While the former has only wasted precious time, the latter has spent quality time. Same principle applies to prayer and every other thing you consider as priority. What makes your time count as quality time is how you spend it.

As a reminder, do not let wish list take the place of real priorities.

KEEPING THE DISTRACTIONS OUT

How do you achieve this? Honestly put together the two lists. Then start by making a decision on what things to ignore in your second true priority list. You see, in most cases we spend time on urgent things. However, urgent things rarely happen to be important. In most cases, they are just loud and urgent, and that's it. They 'know' how to demand our attention in such a way that we have few chances of ignoring them. On the other hand, important things can wait for days, weeks or even years, but if we do not invest our time and attention into them, they slowly die out of our lives. Note that I am not saying that urgent things always have zero importance. If you find yourself having to choose between what is of prime important and what is very urgent, I advise that you delegate the urgent to others so you can keep your focus on the important.

Once you figure out what the distractions are, just make a decision to do away with them and keep them out of your life. This way you'd have plenty of time and strength for your key life activities.

"Things which matter most must never be at the mercy of things which matter least."

Johann Wolfgang von Goethe

"True wisdom is to know what is best worth knowing, and to do what is best worth doing."

Edward Humphrey

DECISION NEVER TO GIVE UP

8. DECISION NEVER TO GIVE UP

"I know what it is to be in need, and I know what it is to have plenty. I have learned the secret of being content in any and every situation, whether well fed or hungry, whether living in plenty or in want. I can do all this through him who gives me strength." - Philippians 4:12-13

Indeed, this is a major decision to take. Unfortunately, there is no true statistics on how many times people failed in their undertakings just because they gave up. Making decisions is easy, following through is the hard part. How many times have you made your resolutions, but failed to come through on them? This is not to discourage you; rather, it is to help you understand how important it is to get through the obstacles on your way.

Starting something is very exciting with the thought of finishing. You come up with plans with prospects in view and you just can't help the burst of euphoria that accompanies the anticipation of reaping the fruit of your efforts. This excitement fuels your zeal as you put your diligent hands on the plow. And then mid-way, it happens. You start to slow down. Droplets of weariness begin to wet your soul. And then in a sweep, the weariness comes upon you in torrents. At that instance you feel like just stopping. Why? Things are not going as planned anymore, with disappointments heaping upon disappointments like they had been lurking in some corner all the while, lying in wait to lay an ambush on you. You never saw it coming.

For many other people, it is not the obstacles that weaken them, rather it realizing how faraway they are from completion of the project. The lose their rear view to see how far into the project we have gone. You get tired, bored, distracted, annoyed, and hindered. You may keep on listing those things capable of stopping you from moving on. But the question is this; have you come this far only so you can give up? You have to decide to not give and be strong in your resolve. This is the time to harness the power of determination that every human is gifted with.

The road to winning is not always exciting. The winner sometimes is the one who is just able to hold on a bit longer than others. See, we have been led to believe wrongly that winning is always an exciting journey, like it feels when watching a Hollywood super-hero movie. Nothing is farther from the truth. Most times, your true victory is not achieved when you finish up something and reap the fruit of success. It is achieved in the struggle, when you get strongly tempted to quit going halfway into your goal. That is the time you need to forge ahead with patience and perseverance. Focus on the course and maintain your commitment. Even when there seems to be no form of encouragement from anywhere or anyone, let your steps be guided by the fact that there is a light at the end of the tunnel.

Do not forget that in the place of struggle lies your victory. This is good motivation to do loads of planning and thinking over before you start anything. However, no matter how well you have planned, do not be too blinded to go back to the drawing board and review your plan if and when you need to. Are you ready to stay committed to your goals no matter what? If yes, then you have to give it all it takes. Believe me, your determination will be tested!

"Never, never, never give up."

Winston Churchill

"Never give up on your dream... because you never know what the Lord can bless you with."

Kelly Rowland

DECISION TO PRIORITIZE

9. DECISION TO PRIORITIZE

"Be very careful, then, how you live – not as unwise but as wise, 16 making the most of every opportunity, because the days are evil." - Ephesians 5:15-16

You have already read the chapter that elaborates the things to ignore and about discovering your true priorities. Now it's time to learn how to make right decisions on your discovered priorities. Here are a few practical tips on how this can be done.

One of the big mistakes people make in trying to prioritize their lives is coming up with long lists of things. If you have ten or more top priorities in your list, you simply get overwhelmed. It may be hard to keep track of many tasks all at the same time. You need to develop exceptional time management skills to avoid getting overwhelmed.

A good starting point in prioritizing is to come up with a shortlist of three to five most important things in you are aiming for. You can always keep them in your head. Focus on these key priorities; think them over time after time. Test them to see if these things are really the key priorities of your life. Weigh them in terms of the benefits they hold. After doing this, make them your goals and take practical steps in pursuing them.

You should start growing the areas of your life that are truly worthy of investing in. Shut out all the distractions. Sometimes, people complain that they have nothing much to invest. But we all are endowed with the same capital - our time! This is actually more valuable all other resources you can think of. It is the ultimate capital. We all have 24 hours to fit our lives in. Start making decisions to invest your time in your key priorities. Follow up with other resources, such as your money, creativity, etc.

This process is not fast-paced. There are steps to follow and indeed, hurdles to cross. You therefore need to make a decision to keep up with steps and observe the details. You should never quit. Get relevant information and guidance from reliable sources. Sources include books, experts and mentors.

So, the ABCs of making decisions to prioritize your life are the following:

- Single out your key priorities
- Limit your list to three to five key positions
- Focus on them
- Turn them into your goals
- Invest in your key priorities

Once you train yourself into going through this ABC once or twice, you develop a useful habit of setting up and pursuing your priorities in life.

DECISION TO CHANGE - AND KEEP CHANGING

10. DECISION TO CHANGE - AND KEEP CHANGING

"Behold, I shew you a mystery; We shall not all sleep, but we shall all be changed." - 1 Corinthians 15:51

One of the reasons for writing this chapter is the common fear most of us deal with - the fear of change. We are afraid of losing the comfort that change may snatch from us. But resisting change is a sign of complacency. Which is why you sometimes find even people who seem to have nothing to lose, do resist change. Imagine an office that decides to change its employees' mode of signing in for work in the morning from analogue to digital and you find people cursing under their breathe in silent rebellion. Instead of welcoming it as a right step towards ensuring transparency, they see it as a new method of witch-hunting. If only their eyes are accustomed to seeing the bright side of things, they would welcome the development as an improved method of ensuring workers' efficiency. If you find yourself feeling attacked by changes of this nature, you really need to check yourself. Are you actually ready for some real possible change that would make your life better?

It is important at this juncture to let you in on some justifications for change.

AVOIDANCE OF STAGNATION

Change is the best cure for stagnation. If there is a collection of water in an area of land, with no inflowing in and outflow, it eventually it becomes a stinking swamp. So, if you feel like your life has become boring, unfruitful and unfulfilling, it is an evidence of a need for a change. Still, most of us have a common fear that things will change for the worse, not for better. It might be so if you do not plan the changes in your life, but go ahead first into them. Take the bull by the horns. Do some planning and do everything you can to engender a positive change and trust God to make it happen.

CHANGE IS NATURAL

If you only take time to think of it, you would realize that change is inevitable. It is natural. From childhood, we keep changing in physical form because we grow bigger. With this comes a change in our reasoning. If physical change is natural, you might as well agree that changes of other forms are inevitable. As we progress in life, we continue to acquire new levels of knowledge from simple to complex. It continues till adulthood when we begin to face serious life challenges. Each moment of challenge that we go through imparts on us and changes us either positively or negatively, depending on how we respond to it. This is why you find some people you have always known as weaklings in times past, surprising us with acts of bravery the next time you see them. Some who were once of noble conduct have now become notorious beings. If you do your research, you will confirm that experiences and the way they reacted to it have left a mark on them and the evidence is that change you have noticed.

Once you settle with the fact that change is natural, you can then decide what kind of change you want to effect in your life- positive or negative.

CHANGE IS A CHANCE

Another great reason to change is to get new chances in life. There are many stories out there, of people who have changed their life occupation in their thirties or even forties and only then they have discovered themselves and their real talents. So, the change opens up the door for new chances in your life. The story is known of a Ray Kroc whose company sold milk shake machines. However, his took a new turn when in 1954 he made contact with the McDonald brothers.

He was supposed to sell the milk shake machine to them. But rather than do just that, he decided to buy a right to a franchise of their company. So much for a change! By 1959, six years later, he had had one two hundred McDonald franchises in the United States. But that only the beginning of a long success story. He would later venture into real estate, buying up properties and leasing them to franchises. From being a selling milk shake machines, this man kept the wheel of change rolling changing, and with every change came a chance to expand, which he definitely explored with attendant results.

If you are consumed with the desire to make a change, especially if this comes with a strong conviction, then take a bold step. Lay your fears to rest. You are probably at the door step to something bigger, but taking that step is your key to that door. You can do away with the fear of change by changing your view of it. The truth is that your fears vanish if you begin to view change as an exciting endeavour and follow up with action.

CHANGE IS A HABIT

You can form a good habit of changing. Once you make the first steps in changing, you discover that most of your fears are not real. For example, you may have a reputation of being crooked and you even get praises for it, since we live in a world where vices are celebrated and virtues are boring. And though you have seen reasons to change, the problem is that you may lose friend. Once you are able to look at things with critical questions, you find the strength to change. Are these people really leading to a safe end in my journey in life? In years to come, will I be proud to tell my children how crooked I have been? These and more are questions to ask. What you are changing is a habit. Do not stop at the initial change. You have to make it a habit to keep changing in order to be better and better. Remember the story of Ray Kroc. That is a classic example of making change a habit.

Complacency is another factor that cripples your habit of changing. Once you get uncritically satisfied with the way you are at present, you will drop very idea of changing. Drawing on the previous examples again: if crookedness is the source of the wealth you have amassed, you can find satisfaction in the fact that you are getting richer after all; not considering the fact our lives do not consist in the abundance of our possessions. Also, being satisfied with initial success would have hindered Ray Kroc from shooting for more. McDonald may not have become the global brand that it is today.

"They always say time changes things, but you actually have to change them yourself."

Andy Warhol

"Stepping onto a brand-new path is difficult, but not more difficult than remaining in a situation, which is not nurturing."

Maya Angelou

DECISION TO TAKE A STAND

11. DECISION TO TAKE A STAND

"When the storm has swept by, the wicked are gone, but the righteous stand firm forever." - Proverbs 10:25

Y ou have to take a stand before the storm to keep on standing after it. What does it mean to take a stand? It means you know what you believe and stand for it. You draw the line somewhere in your life and decide not to cross it. It is like the physical border of a country, which it guards thoroughly. No trespassing is allowed.

Deciding to take a stand for something is very important. You see, if you do not draw that line or set up that border in your life, then you let all kind of things to come into it. Eventually, you risk having no border at all. It is like having the high traffic street going right through your backyard. Once you let different things into your life, parting ways with them becomes really very tough. As the saying goes: If you do not stand for something, you will fall for everything.

One of such things is addiction. It does not really matter what form it takes. Unless you guard your border and take a stand for what is right, the wrong thing would sneak in. It may initially make little mischiefs through you once in a while; but you would hardly notice when it would eventually occupy fully and take over your life. Making a decision to take a stand is all about being responsible.

You must draw a clear line of demarcation between public opinion and your personal conviction. Today, with the great amount of media, too many people get lost. They fall for public opinion and fail to take a stand for what they personally believe is right.

Of course, you do not have to go against the flow always. But there are orientations and values that entirely contradict yours. It is on you to guard you values with diligence regardless of public opinion.

The passage of time has normalized bad things such that they are now viewed as good. Disrespect for elders is one of such. These days, in so homes, talking back at your parents is termed as modernization and sign of a self-emancipated youth. A further example is how the Bible talks about humility and thinking humbly about oneself according to the faith one has. But humility is surely not the most popular word in our culture. On the contrary, psychologists tell you to boost up our self-esteem. And you go on carrying that counsel even when it means trampling on other people. These are perversion of godly principles. This perversion has also applied to many other things, such as sex, marriage, giving, money, pride. And this list can even be made much longer.

As observed, the decision to take a stand for what is right is a hard one. It makes you unpopular, as you start going against the flow. But the good news is that you are promised to keep on standing while others are falling!

"Taking a stand for what you feel right, doesn't always feel good."

Author Unknown

"If you don't stand for something you'll fall for anything..."

Author Unknown

DECISION TO PRAY

12. DECISION TO PRAY

"The LORD is far from the wicked, but he hears the prayer of the righteous." - Proverbs 15:29

Talking of making a decision to pray, we do not talk about as a mere religious practice. True prayer is the life blood of the relationship between God and man. It is not some kind of ritual. It is a two-way communion of two loving hearts. This has to be set straight by way of introduction in order build up the topic of this chapter upon the right notion.

In reality, the decision to pray means starting and keeping up a relationship with God the Almighty. Prayer does not mean petitions only. Just stop and think for a moment: how easy is it for you to ask something from a complete stranger? Most people experience discomfort, when they have to ask for a favour from someone they do not know very well.

Why should this be different with God? How well do you know Him? Is He a complete stranger to you? Why do you think He would listen, when you pray, if you do not have relationships with Him? All these are crucial questions to ponder before you even say your very next prayer. Sometimes, people complain that prayer does not work. But have you just been making requests or you have been having genuine, heartfelt communion with God.

To have a relationship with God, you must regard prayer as a conversation with Him. And the decision to pray would do you no good if you do not do it from the heart. You do know that God is a spirit, which is why our spirit is the medium through which he communicates with us. So, if you have only been moving your mouth in recitation of The Lord's Prayer

67

instead of pouring your heart out to him in truth, then you have not been conversing with Him, you have only been engaging in a fruitless ritual.

Note, there is nothing wrong with asking God for something. And truthfully speaking, it takes God nothing to grant you whatever you ask of Him. Isn't He the creator of the universe and the giver of everything? But it is more important who we become through prayer than what we receive. What we possess may be gone in a split of a second, but who we become through Him is what remains, and with that, what we can achieve is limitless. Remember the story of Job: once rich, then became poor. However, what remained constant was a man who loved good and eschewed evil. And that he remained till God restored him, even in double folds.

This is why it is important that we understand the purpose of prayer and what it can do for us. In prayer, we establish a connection with God. Through this connection, there is a flow of His nature into us. We get to His mind concerning things that concern us so we live according to His will. We become true worshippers through whom He expresses His excellence and might, so that wherever we are, His glory radiates around us for people to see and believe that there is truly a God.

Once the issue of relationship is settled, other things will become a walk over. No father who has a loving relationship with his child will allow such child lack any good thing when He can afford it. It is therefore safe to conclude that sometimes, our prayers do not get answered on time due to lack of cordial relationship with our God.

"Prayer is not asking. It is a longing of the soul. It is daily admission of one's weakness. It is better in prayer to have a heart without words than words without a heart."

Mahatma Gandhi

"Prayer is the key of the morning and the bolt of the evening."

Mahatma Gandhi

DECISION TO REST

13. DECISION TO REST

"Be still, and know that I am God." - Psalm 46:10

Decision to rest is a wise one to make. Our modern life-style tends to get too quick and too stressful. Only few of us are get to fit our lives into the 24 hours we all get every day. Most times, we resort to sacrificing our leisure, family time, important visits and other things just to complete tasks. Rest can be one thing so easy to give up. However, you can only cheat nature for a while.

You can deny your body rest for only as long as it can allow you. Sooner or later, your body will have its rest either by your choice or by force. The reason some people suddenly break down or burn out is not far- fetched. It is an accumulation of stress that the body has endured overtime till it reaches a breaking point. You are not a super-hero after the order of Batman; you are a normal human being created in the like-ness of God. And if God rested on the seventh day after, who are you to try to play a fast one on nature? You probably think you are indispensable because you are the most sort after in your office or best in your field. Permit me to shock you with this brutal fact: the world can do without the best. Have you witnessed the speed with which people get replaced at work after their demise? And why not? The mighty man may have fallen, but the show must go on. God knew the importance of rest; hence He commanded His people to remember the Sabbath and keep it holy. While resting on Sabbath may not be a universal practice today, the whole point of it- rest- has been established.

There are two kinds of rest you can get. One is the rest you plan, the other one is spontaneous. Very many of us agree that getting a spontaneous break in our busy lives is so thrilling. But you cannot rely only on this type of rest. You need to be able to plan your vacation and rest time, as you plan your activities and business or ministry.

This is possible if you make ample rest time part of your priorities. Do not think that you may not have distractions only when you don't work or get busy. You even get more distractions when you are trying to rest. Moreover, our modern culture enforces a certain measure of guilt on people who try to get some good rest doing nothing. Being active is one of the key mottos of our fast pace life.

If you have that problem, just make a change in your mentality and decide to view your rest time as your invest-ment. You invest this time into your health, into your increased creativity, into your family, into your strength, etc.

Again, plan your rest time and do not rely on spontaneous occasions to rest. Make provisions to keep the distraction away. Remember, urgent things are not necessarily important. They are just loud, so they can wait until you rest and restore your strength to deal with them. The decision to rest can be an unlikable idea, because other people may have their plans for your time, too. So, make sure you let them know how firm your decision is and stay disconnected for the time of rest.

"Rest and be thankful."

William Wordsworth

"God never asked us to meet life's pressures and demands on our own terms or by relying upon our own strength. Nor did He demands that we win His favor by assembling an impressive portfolio of good deeds. Instead, He invites us to enter His rest."

Charles R. Swindoll

DECISION TO LEARN

14. DECISION TO LEARN

"Let the wise listen and add to their learning, and let the discerning get guidance." - Proverbs 1:5

The decision to learn is not optional. The world is changing so fast that if you slack at learning, you will be left behind in your field of endeavour, and in no time, your relevance will become questionable. You have to keep pace with the changing world in order to succeed in life. Yesterday's solutions only answer to yesterday's problems. With the advancement pf technology, yesterday's methods cannot address today's rising challenges. Some people are still bent on the carrying on the archaic way of executing jobs. I know of a veteran African journalist who cannot use a computer. He just does not know his way around the use of Microsoft Word. And he is not ready to learn. You may not believe this, but it is true. That means that he has to first write with his pen, then get someone to help him or pay for the service of a typist. What a waste of time, energy and money in a fast-paced world like ours! It is people like him that are getting phased out of relevance with the popularity of blogging, You-Tube and social media. Even the mainstream media houses have realized the need to maintain on-line relevance, which is why they all have social media handles, YouTube channels and mobile apps. If you fail to learn, you will fade away.

Even in the academic world, textbooks that do not get revised regularly can lose its relevance withing 28 months of being published.

Technology and science are advancing at an amazing pace. With the rapid advancement in technology and science, time and space are getting saved by innovations. Which is why machines are replacing humans. The more ATM machines we have, the smaller the number of cashiers we need in banking halls. The same is true about our ever-changing culture, globalization and employment market. Some of our parents used to be proud typists. But that sounds ridiculous to me right now that I am typing the words of this book on my laptop. Many professions get outdated and many new ones come on scene.

The truth is that today, every serious person must be ready to change career every five years. This does not necessarily mean that you leave your profession or the service you render. It simply means your mode of service delivery changing as a result of technological innovations that are making your job easier and you more efficient. The days of mere cab driving are numbered as ride hailing brands such as Uber have emerged. The good thing about learning is that it can be fun, depending on your attitude towards it. You do not have to go back to school and study old and boring way. With the development of interactive Internet technology, knowledge and information have become much more available and fun.

Sometimes, you even get the chance to learn while you earn. Living ready by looking out for new trends and tendencies is essential for success. Still, if you wish to make a headway in life, you need to plan your learning. It's not always necessary you have in-depth knowledge of every new subject or trend you stumble upon. However, there are key areas of knowledge where you can become an expert and open up new opportunities for your personal and business development. That is where you need to plan your learning in. Master it to the level required for you to carry out your professional calling with excellence. Many of us are not computer scientists or software engineers. But an accountant know he needs to be proficient in the use of Microsoft Excel. A modern content writer should be no stranger to Search Engine Optimization especially the area of keywords.

Dedicate a reasonable amount of time a day, or maybe every weekend to learn your course or skill of interest. By doing this, you are developing a good learning habit. Learning becomes more fun and less stressful when it becomes a habit. The feeling of adventure that new things evokes alone should get you excited.

I urge you to make this timely decision today so that your tomorrow self can look back and thank you for the decision that your yesterday self made.

"Any fool can know. The point is to understand."

Albert Einstein

"Tell me and I forget, teach me and I may remember, involve me and I learn."

Benjamin Franklin

DECISION TO GROW

15. DECISION TO GROW

"Instead, speaking the truth in love, we will grow to become in every respect the mature body of him who is the head, that is, Christ. From him the whole body, joined and held together by every supporting ligament, grows and builds itself up in love, as each part does its work." - Ephesians 4:15-16

Growth is intrinsic to our existence as humans. Remember the mention made of growth in the chapter that addresses the decision to change. Growth is progressive change: A change from small to big and big to bigger. A change from good to great. At childhood stage, growth does occur naturally and not by decision. A child naturally grows taller. Children also grow intellectually according to the nurture provided by the world around them. Once an individual begins to transition from childhood to adolescence, growth begins to take occurs in other different dimensions. It goes beyond increase in height and stature. It happens as a function of some internal biological factors. Some hormones begin to activate, engendering the growth of sexual organs and alteration of body shape to a more appealing form. At this stage, your feet get set on the path of personal responsibility. You begin to get information and orientation form different sources including your parents, friends, school, church, street and so on. This information will begin to shape your choices in life in terms of course of study and career, religious and moral conviction, friendship, relationship with the opposite sex and much more. Whatever decisions you make from that moment on will affect the outcome of your life which you are absolutely responsible for. You are not a child anymore, so if you get pushed around by different counsels and opinions that would do you no good, there is no one but yourself to blame for it. You also learn to relate with others, especially the opposite sex with discretion.

So, as you may see, the first step to growing is realizing that now it is your responsibility. See, children grow and develop because it is natural in their case. What to learn is decided for them, not by them.

Once you become an adult, you become responsible for picking the vector of your growth. You aim your life and pick the course for it. Unfortunately, today, many are growing old but not growing up. For most of them, it started from adolescence, when they ought to be growing wiser instead of merely growing taller. Deciding to grow and never stop growing is absolutely up to you.

Growth is an investment you make in yourself. You cannot grow unless you invest. You must be intentional about your growth. This will help you take control and be in charge of your life. Without a deliberate effort at growth, you are likely to accept things that will put you in peril. Because you have not chosen a course of growth, you are just following the crowd. As you follow the crowd, some sort of growth may take place which are full of distractions. This is why some people grow into addictions. These addictions are likely results of neglected responsibility to grow. They are like twisted trees that take the wrong turn at growing. So, you need to learn to invest into your own growth and point it in the right course.

Sometimes, we get too busy to invest time in ourselves. That is why you have to review your priorities and deal with wrong ones. There can only be few things as important in life as investment into one's growth and development. So, as you are making a decision to grow, ensure your priorities are set right and make room and time for growth in your life.

"Happiness is neither virtue nor pleasure nor this thing nor that but simply growth, We are happy when we are growing."

William Butler Yeats

"Intellectual growth should commence at birth and cease only at death."

Albert Einstein

DECISION
TO HELP

16. DECISION TO HELP

"One person gives freely, yet gains even more; another withholds unduly, but comes to poverty." - Proverbs 11:24

The quotes in this chapter seem to contradict so much of the themes of the modern culture. All these ads around us call us to be happy and to please ourselves. The claim: you are worth it! You are the best! Pamper yourself! In any case, helping others may not stand among the top priorities.

You may ask, why should we make this decision? Helping and giving are key spiritual laws. Some people do not believe in spiritual laws. This does not really matter. What is real is real and one person's unbelief will not change it from being real. These laws exist and they work the same way the law of gravity works. You may claim you do not believe the law of gravity, but that disbelief would not help you if you get up on a high tower and jump down.

The good thing about the law of giving is that once you discover it, you can use it for your good and that of others around you. If you are new to giving and helping, then you may experience certain discomfort prima facie. Some people are stingy, while others feel embarrassed as they try to help others. So you think of helping someone, but then you ask, "What if they do not need my help? What if they are mean to me?"

Making a decision to help means you need to keep away those thoughts. You know, people will be mean to you. People may not always be thankful for your help. More often than not, people under distress can even be rude to you. They may have experienced too much pain to be polite. Still, all these things are not excuses for not helping others. You are not helping just so you can receive thanks and appreciation. People need something, but you have and can afford to spare, then go on and give. Do you not also receive help from people too sometimes? It may not even be material. The point is that we can render help just as we may need help too. An act of kindness is something you do for the good of it. So, once you make a decision in your heart to help people, you should couple this decision with another one: make a decision not to expect anything good back from them.

Giving and helping is another great investment you can make in your life. You give away and free up the room in your life to receive something new. If you feel like your life has become dull or stale, start giving. If you see a need in your life, find someone who is even needier and start giving and helping. This opens up the help door for you and help will come into your life. God has His amazing and rich sources to provide you with help in the time of need.

"The purpose of life is not to be happy. It is to be useful, to be honorable, to be compassionate, to have it make some difference that you have lived and lived well."

Ralph Waldo Emerson

"No one is useless in this world who lightens the burdens of another."

Charles Dickens

DECISION TO GET TRAINED

17. DECISION TO GET TRAINED

"For this command is a lamp, this teaching is a light, and correction and instruction are the way to life." - Proverbs 6:23

The decision to get trained differs from the decision to learn. You can learn from the host of books or other sources of information out there. But it is most effective when a person trains another. While reading helps you understand the principles and rules of engagement, training exposes you to real life practice under the guidance of someone who has done it over and again and gained expertise. Bulk of your success depends on your trainer.

A good trainer is able to establish a connection between him/her and the audience or students. They become the magnets, which makes training fun, engaging and productive.

View your training as your investment. Never stop with your professional training. Even if you have reached a certain level in your profession, you still can become better. So, look for opportunities to get trained and make a decision to get trained. Search for interesting people who know much more than you do. Get them to train you.

Invest time in your training and be committed. Sometimes, training can be tough. It can be frustrating, too. You may have thought that you know it all. Once you start the training course, you discover how many things you have missed. In fact, you can feel your ego bruised because your unknown inadequacies get exposed. But you need to drop your ego and learn from someone who has been there and has beaten many odds. I am not sorry for being brutally honest, there is really no better way to say this for it to ring true in your mind. Your trainer in this scenario has nothing to lose, it is you who may stand the risk of underachievement due to being less competent than you could have been. Press on and do not quit. Yes, you may feel not so comfortable for a while, but it is for your good at the end of the day.

Aside from professional training, you should also decide to pursue trainings on personal development. This can be very informal. You just need a mentor- someone who has led a successful personal life with results. You see someone who has a healthy relationship with his family and friends, and this is something you know you need, get close to such person and discover how he has maintained stability in his relationship. You would be amazed at the wealth of lessons such an individual can teach you on emotional intelligence, honesty, effective communication and much more.

While these things may not seem to be urgent or essential, taking your time to develop yourself in these areas will translate to growth in the long run. So, making a decision to take a training course in an area of interest to you is instrumental to leading a better life.

"I hated every minute of training, but I said, 'Don't quit. Suffer now and live the rest of your life as a champion.'"

Muhammad Ali

"You are your greatest asset. Put your time, effort and money into training, grooming, and encouraging your greatest asset."

Tom Hopkins

DECISION TO BE A READER

18. DECISION TO BE A READER

"For wisdom will come into your heart, and knowledge will be pleasant to your soul; discretion will watch over you, understanding will guard you." - Proverbs 2:10-11

In the 21st century, acquisition of knowledge often comes through reading. Without doubt, knowledge and success are connected. Not many people can actually boast of being successful without knowledge and continuous learning.

Reading remains one of the most effective yet probably unappreciated self-development tools. It has immeasurable benefits. Reading is a long- standing tradition that can and will never become outdated. And it is this indestructible nature of knowledge that should inform your decision to read this book and a body of other edifying literature.

Are you aware that reading has a lot of therapeutic and social benefits? Reading helps in the following ways:

- It enhances your smartness and intelligence
- It helps you acquire wisdom
- It makes you attractive to others, as people tend to gravitate someone they can learn from.
- It helps you reduce the risk of hypertension and other health problems
- It enhances your memory

There are a whole lot of other benefits of reading so this is one good decision to make in one's life.

Reading gets you to the top in life. People naturally tend to look up to someone from whom they can get answers to real life puzzles and solutions to challenges. Those that others turn to for answers and directions are those who have acquired wisdom by walking their eyes through the pages of quality books. This holds true everywhere from office, to church, community and even the home. This is why all great leaders are said to have something in common - they read avidly.

Surveys have revealed severally that CEOs read an average of five books in a month- that is sixty in a year. In fact, more inspiring is finding that a notable number of the most prosperous leaders in history fondly read at least a book every single day.

But what kind of books do they read? There are different kinds of books including those that indoctrinate you into false beliefs. This class of people mentioned read books that concern their field and several other books on different subject to broaden their world of knowledge and help them reach higher grounds.

You just cannot be an exceptional leader, if you are not an ardent reader. You might be thinking to yourself that you have no aspiration to occupy any position of leadership. That is a very erroneous line of thought. Leadership is not all about position and title. True leadership is the ability to see ahead, analyze different perspectives, provide unquestionable answers, influence sound decisions and effect positive changes. Do you need a corner office with a name tag at the door to do all of that? The qualities mentioned are skills that books will help you acquire.

"Never trust anyone who has not brought a book with them."

Lemony Snicket, Horseradish: Bitter Truths You Can't Avoid

"We read to know that we are not alone."

William Nicholson

DECISION TO READ THE WORD

19. DECISION TO READ THE WORD

"Get wisdom, get understanding; do not forget my words or turn away from them." - Proverbs 4:5

Some people do not view the decision to read the Bible as something important. And without them noticing, it is doing a serious disservice to their lives. Other people think that the Bible is an old and outdated book. They often ask, "What good can reading the Bible do for the inhabitants of the modern world?" Mostly, people think so because of their ignorance.

So, what are some reasons to base your decision to read the Word upon? Let's take a look at just few of them here.

THE BIBLE IS THE MANUAL OF LIFE

When we get new set of equipment, we need to learn how to operate it. Then we turn to the maker's manual for details. Bible is the Maker's manual of humans. God created us and He is the only One who has the ultimate capacity to decide how we are to live our lives. And since we cannot see Him- just like we do not necessarily get to see a product's manufacturer- He has offered the Bible as a manual for us.

Many people get into various troubles in life that are beyond human explanation, and they do not know the way out. They do not even know how to respond. Why not turn to the source and discover the secrets that you have been hiding from yourself? Get you hands on the manual and discover how to rightly navigate your way thorough life. Bible holds the wisdom.

Getting knowledge is not enough to succeed in life. Knowledge is good, but wisdom is better. Wisdom teaches you how to use the knowledge you possess to attain success. Ultimate wisdom belongs to God, an we can access it from His word-the Bible. Bible changes your mentality. You get transformed through mind renewal as Apostle Paul wrote.

When you decide to read the Word, you get the paradigm shift and learn the thinking patterns of God.

THE BIBLE IS PRACTICAL

Bible is not a history book. Yes, it contains tons of true historic facts. But that is not the key goal of the authorship of the Bible. It is a life book. And it is highly practical. It can give you the wisdom and understanding for your daily life. Yes, the world has changed, meaning it has become more techno-cratic. But the truth of God's word remains the same forever. It is timeless. The decision to read the Word gives your life a solid foundation. When everything else in the world looks unstable, you get the unmovable rock to build your life upon.

"A thorough knowledge of the Bible is worth more than a college education."

Theodore Roosevelt

"Within the covers of the Bible are the answers for all the problems men face."

Ronald Reagan

DECISION TO BE COMMITTED TO A COURSE

20. DECISION TO BE COMMITTED TO A COURSE

"Commit your work to the Lord, and your plans will be established." - Proverbs 16:3

Many find it challenging to staying on course after making decisions. There is only word for this: indiscipline. There are so many distractions in the world, which tend to steer us off a chosen course. Still, making a decision to stay on course can be the difference between failure and success.

You already know that every coin has two sides and you may object that sometimes staying committed is not the best thing you can do. Some people say that there is the eleventh commandment, which is "Blessed are flexible, for they will not be broken". So, how can you reconcile these two seemingly contradicting truths - staying committed and being flexible? In reality, they do fall perfectly in line with each other.

You see, you need to put forth efforts and take time to pick your course. It should not be a quick decision. You need to think well over it and define the desired outcomes or destination of the chosen course. You do not stop there; you must also follow it through if you wish to get to the desired destination.

Granted, on your journey, you will encounter reasons to make tons of smaller decisions, such as adopting and modifying your approaches, your timing and a lot of other success determinants. This is where flexibility comes in. It is like driving and walking. You have just one destination, but there are many alternative routes. In fact, you cannot hope to stay on course unless you stay flexible on the way.

Life is changing and it demands people to be flexible. Being rigid throughout the entire course may end up in breakdown instead of attaining your goal. So, it is wise to be flexible wherever and whenever it is necessary, but without compromising your chosen course and goals.

To stay on course, you must be wise and patient and flexible enough to maneuver through obstacles.

"Great changes may not happen right away, but with effort even the difficult may become easy."

Bill Blackman

"Obstacles are those frightful things you see when you take your eyes off your goal."

Henry Ford

DECISION TO KNOW THE TRUTH

21. DECISION TO KNOW THE TRUTH

"Buy the truth and do not sell it - wisdom, instruction and insight as well." - Proverbs 23:23

The Bible tells us that the truth will set us free. The truth saves your soul, but there are situations when it can save your life, too.

We should first define what truth is. One of the essential characteristics of truth is stability. Truth does not change with time. It is different from fact. While fact can be subject to logic (a scientifically explicable cause and effect situation), truth is self-proven. For example, it is a fact that a child is formed only after a sperm comes in contact with an ovum; but the truth is that Jesus was born without the contribution of a sperm. It is timeless. It does not grow old in the modern age of technology.

Knowing the truth is not enough. Once you make a decision to know the truth, you need to make another decision to accept or reject it. For truth is radical. There is no compromise with it. It is like the gravity law - you can break it and die or you can accept it and fly!

The truth always remains true. Circumstances may change. Opinions may change, but truth lies unreachable by these things. It cannot be altered by them.

See, the recent decades seem to have changed the world and thrown it into avoidable chaos. People have changed opinions on many things and have shown the truth the door out of their lives. This happens when they are not comfortable with it anymore. They now need an alternative opinion to endorse their self-seeking idiosyncrasies. Making a decision to know the truth and stick with it requires laying down selfish desires at the feet of conscience. One truth for example is that honesty is the best policy- a secular credence to the commandment, 'thou shall not lie'. But we find a lot of people inflating prices of items to procure in the office, and they can justify it with a genuine and pressing need. When they get caught, this justification cannot save them in the face of the law. The good news is that if you stand for the truth, it stands for you, too. It becomes the foundation of your life.

Things may get tough midway, but truth makes you the winner just because it proves to be true at the end!

Another characteristic is that the truth is wise. However, you need to be able to glance at it from the right angle. If you view the truth from the worldly point of view, it seems like foolishness. Remember, truth is eternal and brings ever-lasting wisdom, which sometimes cannot be seen through a prism of the moment.

"In a time of universal deceit - telling the truth is a revolutionary act."

George Orwell

"Whoever is careless with the truth in small matters cannot be trusted with important matters."

Albert Einstein

DECISION TO LIVE AND NOT MERELY EXIST

22. DECISION TO LIVE AND NOT MERELY EXIST

"I cry out to God Most High, to God who fulfills his purpose for me." - Psalm 57:2

You know, many of us get fooled in respect of living and enjoying our lives. The world tells us that we have to possess so many things to live and not merely exist. We need to get good jobs, lots of money, nice house, nice cars, we need to be popular, famous or important to live and enjoy the life. Surely, these things are good things, especially if acquired by legitimately. Yet, these things are not the ultimate definer of living. At best, they are objects of personal gratification.

This is why even after getting all of these things, we still keep on feeling miserable. We set new goals, we put together new lists and pursue them. So, when is it a good time for you to be happy and to start enjoying your life? When will you really get fulfilled? Whatever you are doing now, can you picture a future in which you will look back at this moment and breath in the air of satisfaction? S pointed out earlier, we get fooled in this respect of possessing and accumulating material things. The truth is that living is really defined by how much impact you make. The past is gone and who knows what kind of future we have and if we have it? Now is the time to start thinking of the very purpose for which you came to this earth. Jesus Christ was not one of the rich guys of his time, yet he truly lived on earth because of the impact he made which will continue to speak till He returns. The rich man in his parable on the other hand merely existed because his life was all about himself. His wealth was for his own gratification.

There is a special gift God has put in you and He expects you to give expression to it and thereby impact your word.

Running after material possession alone will only keep you bondage. But putting a smile on faces with what you have, bring hope to broken souls, and contributing to the peace of your environment are the markers of how well you have lived.

Make your walk on this earth significant enough to make your footprint indelible on the sands of time and your name written in gold in hearts of people.

> "The purpose of life is not to be happy. It is to be useful, to be honorable, to be compassionate, to have it make some difference that you have lived and lived well."

Ralph Waldo Emerson

> "You were put on this earth to achieve your greatest self, to live out your purpose, and to do it fearlessly."

Steve Maraboli, Life, the Truth, and Being Free

DECISION TO ATTEND CHURCH REGULARLY

23. DECISION TO ATTEND CHURCH REGULARLY

"...not forsaking the assembling of ourselves together, as is the manner of some, but exhorting one another, and so much the more as you see the Day approaching." - Hebrews 10:25

If you are a believer, then attending church regularly should be part of your lifestyle. Talking about church, it should be understood that that it is beyond a building. Church is the body of Christ, a fellowship of people gathered together to commune with the Almighty. If you belong to Christ, you should love this fellowship and being part of it at all times.

It's funny that sometimes people say they love God, and yet have a hard time loving church people. How can this be possible? Yes, of course, loving God is much easier, than loving people. God is perfect and people are not. But unless you can learn to love the perfect God in imperfect people, your faith and love will remain incomplete.

Let's take a look at some of the reasons you need to make a decision to attend church regularly:

➤ CHURCH IS THE PLACE TO BE BORN AGAIN

Of course, we can get born again in any place and at any time. But church is an assembly of His people. The Bible charges us to not fail to be in the assembly of brethren. There is power in fellowship. God is always present wherever two or three are gathered in His name. Therefore, it is only just right to come and seek Him in church

➤ CHURCH IS THE PLACE OF GROWTH

We grow by attending church regularly. This growth is not only spiritual and caused by prayer and hearing the Word;

it is also a personal growth. You meet different people, take up responsibilities and make commitments. All these greatly contribute to your personal growth.

➤ CHURCH IS A PLACE TO BE SERVED

In church, we get our needs met. It is the place to get ministered to and have God work through other people in the church to meet our needs.

➤ CHURCH IS A PLACE TO SERVE

While it is good to make a decision to attend church regularly to get refilled and to receive, it is even better to make a commitment to come to church and serve or give. To give is a greater blessing than to receive. God loves givers. Church is the best place to become one.

➤ CHURCH IS A PLACE TO ENJOY

A good church is the place to enjoy your life, enjoy God and enjoy your friends.

➤ CHURCH IS THE PLACE TO STAY IN FELLOW-SHIP

It is hard to stay a strong believer if you get fellowship only with unbelievers. The possibility is high of these people to influence you to turn your heart away from God. That is why making a decision to attend church regularly is so important. You get fellowship with likeminded people, who believe in God and love God. It keeps you strong in faith.

"You can be committed to Church but not committed to Christ, but you cannot be committed to Christ and not committed to church."

Joel Osteen

"Anyone who is to find Christ must first find the church. How could anyone know where Christ is and what faith is in him unless he knew where his believers are?"

Martin Luther

DECISION TO BE CREATIVE

24. DECISION TO BE CREATIVE

"For you created my inmost being; you knit me together in my mother's womb." - Psalm 139:13

Every human has a talent. God is the Creator, and He made us in His own image and likeness. This means we have also been made creative. Creativity is in our essence. Everyone is creative. Only some people have discovered their creative abilities and let it out, while others are either not observant enough to identify it or too insecure to give it expression.

Why should you make a decision to be creative? For one, you need it to be happy and fulfilled in life. If you do not give your creativity a chance, you will doom an essential item in you to stay buried deep down inside. How can you expect to be happy after you have buried part of yourself alive? Impossible!

Another more practical reason to be creative is in order to succeed in life. What you are a natural at propels you to greatness faster than what you learned. I believe all the great people would ascribe their success in some measure to their creativity, as well as to their hard work.

Now, how do you make a decision to be creative? Scientists believe that creativity is something that comes out of our subconscious. Can you do something practical to help it happen? Yes, you can. Scientists have discovered that our minds come up with creative solutions when we get relaxed and completely set our thoughts off the problems we've been trying to solve.

So, if you need a creative solution, get focused on your problem. But then take time to relax. Do whatever helps you unwind- take a shower if you need, make coffee break, go for a drive, etc. Good relaxation time often boosts your creativity.

Get inspired. This is the next step to boosting your creativity. Know yourself. Take time to understand what inspires you the most. Some people get inspired by the beauty of nature. Others get inspired by nice smells. You may also get inspired by ideas of other people. Detect your inspiration source and take time to get inspired. You cannot hope to get something, unless you give. Give your subconscious some food for inspiration.

Do something you love doing. Our busy world has set up strict limits on what it considers useful and reasonable. Sometimes, the most enjoyable things do not fall under that description. Yet, you have no reason to dispose of from your life those things you love just because people around you disregard it. Get a hobby. Do what you love. Recall your childhood and remember something you enjoyed doing the most. What were your dreams then? It's time to make them come true.

> "Creativity is just connecting things. When you ask creative people how they did something, they feel a little guilty because they didn't really do it, they just saw something. It seemed obvious to them after a while. That's because they were able to connect experiences they've had and synthesize new things."
>
> **Steve Jobs**

> "An essential aspect of creativity is not being afraid to fail."
>
> **Edwin Land**

DECISION TO
BE MATURE

25. DECISION TO BE MATURE

"Do not be wise in your own eyes; fear the Lord and shun evil." - Proverbs 3:7

It seems like maturity is something inevitable in our lives. As we grow old, we ought to grow up as well. Unfortunately, not everyone gets to grow up. This is why you sometimes see an elderly man acting like an adolescent. Some people have not trashed their aggressive conduct even as they age. So, you sometimes you see a sixty-year-old man or woman still acting like a hooligan, responding with physical attack when in conflict. Maturity is of great value in that it helps you make right decisions and live a better life. It keeps you from repeating the mistakes of your youth.

However, maturity is a choice. You have to make a decision to be mature. You were not just born that way. So, let us take a look at some practical maturity tips you can follow:

➤ GROW YOUR SELF-MOTIVATION

A mature person is marked by their ability to motivate themselves. They do not need other people to come and tell them what to do. They know their responsibilities or aspirations and motivate themselves to move and pursue their goals.

➤ LEARN TO LISTEN TO OTHER PEOPLE

Talk, talk and talk - this is not a sign of a maturity. One of the abilities you need to develop to mature is the ability to listen. You need to master the skill of becoming an attentive and zealous listener.

➤ OWN UP TO YOUR MISTAKES

Shame or disapproval is part of the things immature people dread the most. Maturity knows how to own up to mistakes and analyze them. There is no use getting defensive trying to justify those mistakes. We all make mistakes. They are natural part of our lives. But if you can own up to mistakes, you can analyze them and learn from them.

> MAKE ALLOWANCES

We all need plenty of allowances to be made for us. No one is perfect. So, put away your judge mantle and get clothed in humility and acceptance. Cover up the mistakes of others without being hard on them.

> LEARN MANAGEMENT

Making a decision to be mature, you need to learn how to manage yourself, your time, your efforts, your resources, etc. You need to know how to handle these things and how to rule your life.

> PICK THE RIGHT FRIENDS

These people do not have to be perfect. But it is good to associate with those who share your values and your ideas. If your friends have high aspirations, they become the source of motivation and inspiration for you.

> BECOME A GIVER

A mature person is not looking to receive. Yes, we all have to receive in order to give. But a mature person knows the balance between these two. They know that giving initiates the receiving cycle in your life.

"Maturity is achieved when a person postpones immediate pleasures for long-term values."

Joshua L. Liebman

"To make mistakes is human; to stumble is commonplace; to be able to laugh at yourself is maturity."

William Arthur Ward

DECISION TO BE WISE

26. DECISION TO BE WISE

"The wise inherit honor, but fools get only shame." - Proverbs 3:35

Wisdom is a word used by all and sundry. But what does it actually mean? Wisdom is simply knowing the right thing to do and doing it. Most of us can make a decision and after seeing the result, assert that the decision was wise. Other times, the result makes us realize that our decision was foolish. But there are ways to determine ahead of time what is wise and what is not? Let us take a look at few things that might come handy if you have decided to be wise.

➤ AVOID BEING IN HASTE

In most cases, hasty decisions are the worst. When you are in haste, you do not have time to think things over. This means, you do not make the decisions, but rather allow circumstances or other people to make them for you. That is just folly, nothing more. So, whenever there is haste, there are high chances of making a wrong decision.

➤ CONSULT

Get advice from others. There is nothing shameful about asking people for their opinions or advice. They may just have that right knowledge or experience you need to move to the next level in life.

➤ GET THE RIGHT INFORMATION

You see, there is no way you can make right decision based on wrong information. So, take time to gather the right data upon which to base your decision. Verify the authenticity of the data that inform your actions and decisions.

> ‣ UNDERSTAND

It is unwise to react to or act upon your first impressions. Here is an example. You may come in touch with an irate individual who cries or screams. If you jump to making conclusions about that person based on your first impressions, it is very likely your conclusions would be wrong.

People deal with various situations differently, and in most cases, they have good reasons to behave the way they do. Sometimes, we get offended by a behavior that has nothing to do with us. It was triggered by incident or situation and we just accidentally encountered it. So, take time to understand people or situations and to look at their core essence before you make up your mind about them.

Wisdom is crucial to the outcome of every of our engagements, endeavours and relationships. It renews hope, prevents disasters, solves problems, builds and mends relationships and even saves lives. So, whatever you have decided upon at the moment, include the decision to get wisdom with it.

"A good head and a good heart are always a formidable combination."

Nelson Mandela

"A little knowledge that acts is worth infinitely more than much knowledge that is idle."

Khalil Gibran

DECISION TO BE CONTENT

27. DECISION TO BE CONTENT

"If you find honey, eat just enough - too much of it, and you will vomit." - Proverbs 25:16

Very many people wish that things flow as they have planned. They always want to have everything they want, every time. That is one of the factors that contribute to the number of unhappy people on earth. Your ability to be content with what you have determines your happiness in life. If you learn to be content under any circumstance, you will have a better control over your life. Then, your happiness will be in your own hands and not in things you have or desire.

Apostle Paul wrote that it is huge gain to be content. Contentment is not something you get born with. You develop this ability. So, what are the practical things you can do to help your decision to be content? Let's take a look at some of them here.

➤ ENDEAVOR TO SEE THE BRIGHT SIDE OF THINGS

It is hard to be content or happy, if your head is preoccupied with negative thoughts. There are many situations wherein changing things become ostensibly impossible. But in most cases, you can change your point of view on them.

It is a mentality shift you need to make. Train yourself to see the positive in everything. Every coin has two sides. Most situations have something good to offer. However, we would miss the good should we fail to see and recognize the positive.

➤ CHOOSE TO ENJOY EVERY MOMENT OF YOUR LIFE

Some people live in the past. Others live in the future. The thought of a bad past brings hurt and regrets. The thought of an uncertain future breeds anxiety. But the power to bring yourself to live in the present is in your hands. Living in the present and enjoying it to the fullest is a choice that brings contentment. Learn to focus on each moment of your life. It's the only moment you have! The past is off your hands and the future is not yet within your reach. There are so many pleasant gifts around you if you would give thought to them: a beautiful family, great friends, a peaceful environment, and ultimately a God to set your hope on in case you lack any of these. Be the decider of your own happiness. Live in the moment and be free.

➤ LEARN TO TRIGGER POSITIVE EMOTIONS

Sometimes, human emotions seem to be as uncontrollable as the wind. But in many cases, you can control your emotions. So, if you are willing to, you can trigger positive emotions. Some people feel good being exposed to certain smell. Others enjoy music, nature, art, etc. Take time to find the things that trigger your positive emotions and use them daily to stay content with life.

Hopefully, these simple things would help you to make a decision to be content and start enjoying your daily life.

"True contentment is a thing as active as agriculture. It is the power of getting out of any situation all that there is in it. It is arduous and it is rare."

Gilbert K. Chesterton

"The world is full of people looking for spectacular happiness while they snub contentment."

Doug Larson

DECISION TO BE GENEROUS

28. DECISION TO BE GENEROUS

"One person gives freely, yet gains even more; another withholds unduly, but comes to poverty." - Proverbs 11:24

There is more to generosity than giving. People may give for various reasons. They may be motivated by others or by circumstances. But a generous person is self-motivated in giving.

One of the distinctive traits of a generous person is their ability to see where the need is and meet that need. Generosity is not an inborn quality. No one is born generous. It is the decision we make that prompts that change in us. So, how do you become a generous person?

➤ TRAIN YOUR EYES AND EARS

When you interact with other people, you should train yourself to see where their needs are. If you make a decision to be generous, you should not sit and wait for someone to come and ask for help. You make the first step first — go ahead and look for needs with the hope of meeting them as appropriate.

➤ CONSIDER THE RIPPLE EFFECTS

A generous person gives freely because they know the ripple effect of giving. When you cast even a small stone into the water, it causes ripples. These ripples are much larger than the stone. The same applies to giving. Even if you give something small, it can elicit life-transforming change around you - in your life or the lives of other people. Generous giving is like sowing. It produces fruit in people's lives.

➤ GET IN THE HABIT

It may not come easily at first. It is like starting a rusty engine. It does not work smoothly at first, but then you rub it with oil and you make it run for a while. Then it starts working more and more smoothly. That is how you make a decision to be generous. It may be hard at first, but after you practice generosity for a while, it becomes easier.

➤ FIND GOOD EXAMPLES TO FOLLOW

You may get inspired to be generous. You may see how other people have changed the world by their generosity. Then to follow their footprints becomes easier for you. So, find such inspiring examples and follow those people with your words and actions.

➤ GET ENGAGED

Giving something to people you do not know may not be very exciting. It may seem foolish in some cases. So, get engaged. Start your own generosity projects. Get excited about them. Go ahead first into carrying them out and give with joy. What is special about this is that it is the true test of generosity - giving to people who may never get the chance to pay you back maybe not even a chance to meet you and say thank you.

Real generosity toward the future lies in giving all to the present.

Albert Camus

Real generosity is doing something nice for someone who will never find out.

Frank A. Clark

DECISION TO KNOW YOUR PLACE IN LIFE

29. DECISION TO KNOW YOUR PLACE IN LIFE

"There is a time for everything, and a season for every activity under the heavens." - Ecclesiastes 3:1

We live in a world driven by such mottos as "you can do more", "you can make it", "live the dream", etc. These mottos are good, but sometimes they play bad tricks on us. Every activity has its proper place and limits. The same applies to every individual. We all are limited beings, and where danger lies with most of us is denying these boundaries and stepping out of our place in life.

Now, most of us do not really like the word "limit", but we all have it. Acknowledging our limits is an exercise of humility. When you know your time and your place in life, you become humble and happy. Aspirations are great, but when you aspire beyond the God-set limit, you fall into the trap of pride.

That is the same trap devil got himself into. He refused to know his place and time; he refused to know his limits and aspired too high. Pride always comes before the fall. But humility precedes glory.

Now, there is one important thing to discuss when it comes to knowing your place in life. There is no shame in being humble. When you recognize your limits - the limits of your personality and your abilities - you preserve your self-respect. There is nothing disrespectful in bowing down before the Lord and acknowledging His plan and purpose for your life.

Humility has no humiliation in it. Plus, humility keeps you safe. When you know your place in life, your life becomes purposeful and meaningful. When you acknowledge your limits, your life becomes safe.

Now, knowing your limits does not mean you have to forsake your dream. Here is a good example. Men always wanted to fly. It was a big dream and it was meant to come true. However, we had to acknowledge our limits and understand that we cannot possibly fly using the power of our muscles. We had to recognize gravity law and humble ourselves. But then we discovered the law of aerodynamics and found a way to fly.

That's how it works. Knowing your place in life and recognizing your limits may usher you into a realm of safe and realistic fulfillment of dreams. All things are possible with God, but this also means that not all things are possible with men. You need to humble yourself by recognizing your own limits to resort to the power of Omnipotent God and dive into His limitless abilities.

"The difference between stupidity and genius is that genius has its limits."

Albert Einstein

"Once we accept our limits, we go beyond them."

Albert Einstein

DECISION
TO BELIEVE

30. DECISION TO BELIEVE

"For the word of the Lord is right and true; he is faithful in all he does." - Psalm 33:4

The Bible verse above states that God is faithful in all He does. In other words, God is full of faith! We are created in His image and likeness. It is only natural for human beings to be full of faith. We cannot live by thoughts alone or by emotions only. People live by faith.

That is not just a fancy or groundless statement. Reasoning is not enough for us to live on. Here is a very simple example. Do you use elevators? If you do, you use them by faith. You do not know that any given elevator would lift you up to a certain floor. You step inside of it in faith. You believe it would bring you there safely. There is no strict knowledge - it's a matter of believing in something you do not know.

Most of the things we do in our lives are done by believing. Those are common daily life things. We eat by faith; we move by faith; we drive by faith, etc.

However, lots of that believing is done subconsciously. The difficulties start when we have to believe consciously. Many people seem to have hard times believing in God. They have to make their choice to believe in Him. However, many smart people do not find believing worthy. They think believing is a prerogative of ignorant people. They believe themselves to be too smart for believing. Does that sound funny to you?

The truth is, quite a number of people lack real proof of their cleverness. They just believe themselves to be clever. But they find it shameful and unworthy of their mind to believe in God or in anything else. That is when people try to substitute believing with arguments or debates.

The problem is that faith bears fruit, while debates don't. Faith moves you to action - as it opens up a door for you to the supernatural realm. Debate on the other hand keeps you focused on natural, keeping your mind on your doubts alone.

Making a decision to be a believer is a good step in life. It does not necessarily have to be a decision to believe in God - though believing in God is the best decision to consider in life. Still, believing prepares you for new things. You are able to see something new - which doubt has no eyes for and can never pick. When you believe, you begin to see new opportunities in life. It gives you vital advantage over none believing people. So, make a decision to believe, but find firm foundation for your faith.

"A man lives by believing something: not by debating and arguing about many things."

Thomas Carlyle

"We are born believing. A man bears beliefs as a tree bears apples."

Ralph Waldo Emerson

DECISION TO BE CONSISTENT

31. DECISION TO BE CONSISTENT

"My heart is set on keeping your decrees to the very end." - Psalm 119:112

D ecision to be consistent is very important. You cannot hope to get anything done unless you are able to keep on going in that direction for a while. Some things take just few hours or few days to accomplish. Others take years, decades or even an entire lifetime to get done. Consistency is something that helps you to arrive at your destination sooner or later.

Consistency is fueled by determination. Once you get determined to get something done, you become consistent in a bid to attain your goals. Consistency is your ability to keep going in the same direction for a long time. The more consistent you are in your efforts, the better results you get.

How do you go about the decision to be consistent? Let us take a look at some steps to make.

> SLOW DOWN

If you wish to get things done quickly, you may ruin your consistency. Some things take time to get them done. For instance, you cannot hope to shed pounds over the night. You need to be consistent in exercising and eventually you attain the desired result.

So, slow down a bit. We live in a fast-paced world where instant response is the order of the day. We get instant communication, fast food, fast transportation, etc. And we tend to lose patience and fail to be consistent. So, we tend to apply this trendy things that take a process that is not automated. We must make a turn form this approach and embrace the process. Imbibe the virtue of patience and press on.

➤ COME UP WITH YOUR SCHEDULE

Consistency has to be planned. It does not happen accidentally or by inspiration. You have to plan it. Plan your regular actions for attaining your goals. Make regular efforts to attain them.

➤ CREATE HABITS THAT FACILITATE YOUR CONSISTENCY

Habits are the things we do automatically. It's an easy way to be consistent. If you know that some things take months or years to get done, create some useful habits. For instance, if you plan to stay fit or become fit, you need to get in a habit of daily exercising. Then you stop having to resort to your will power and make yourself exercise. You start doing it automatically.

➤ GET SUPPORT

People that surround you can either help you to be consistent and to attain your goals or tear you down. So, making a decision to be consistent will require you picking the right people to associate with.

These simple tips would help you get on the right track and carry out your decision to be consistent.

> "I've learned from experience that if you work harder at it, and apply more energy and time to it, and more consistency, you get a better result. It comes from the work."

Louis C. K.

> "Consistency, madam, is the first of Christian duties."

Charlotte Bronte

OTHER BOOKS BY
ABRAHAM GREAT

365 Brilliant English Words

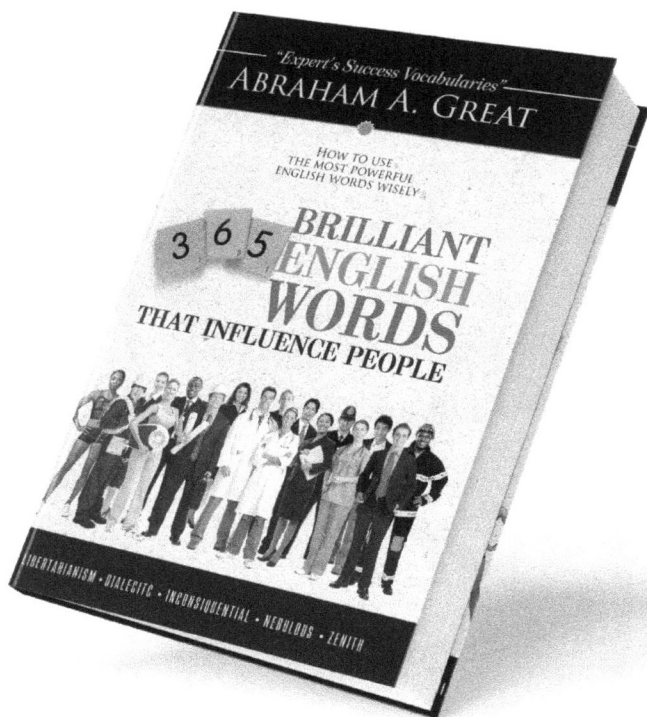

OTHER BOOKS BY
ABRAHAM GREAT

52 Proofs of the existence of God

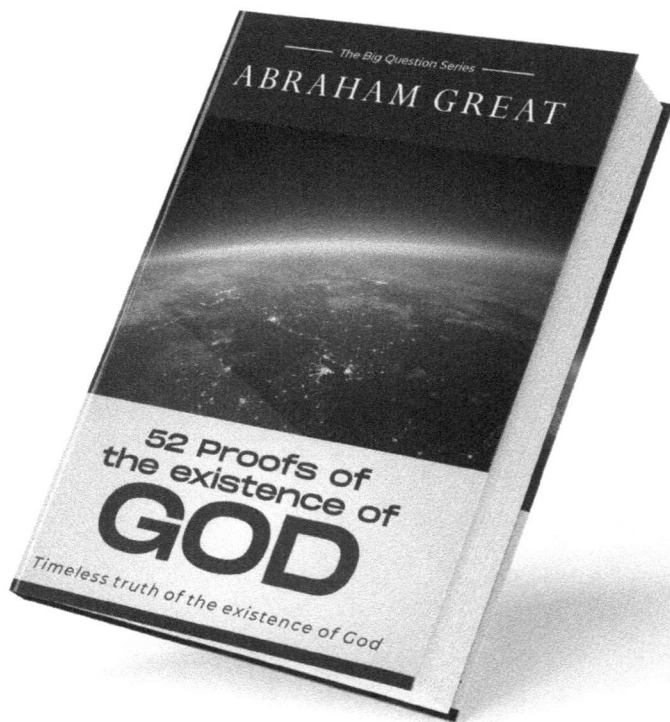

OTHER BOOKS BY
ABRAHAM GREAT

31 Decisions that make a person of value

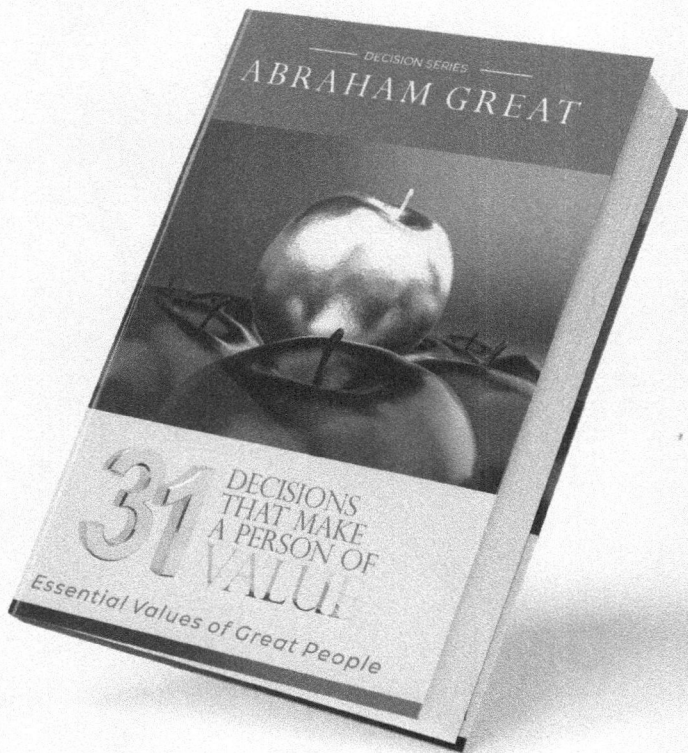

OTHER BOOKS BY

ABRAHAM GREAT

∙

31 Decisions that make a man of value

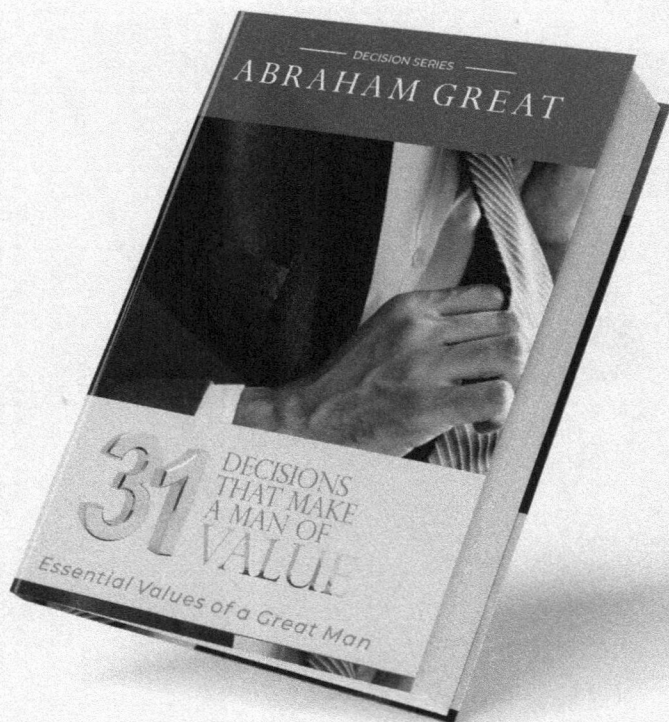

OTHER BOOKS BY
ABRAHAM GREAT

31 Decisions that make a Woman of Value

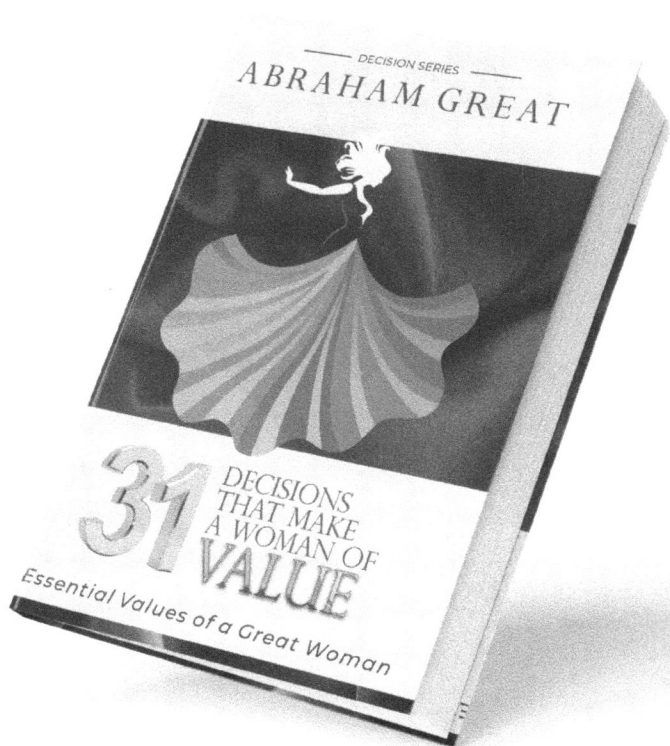

OTHER BOOKS BY
ABRAHAM GREAT

Understanding Values

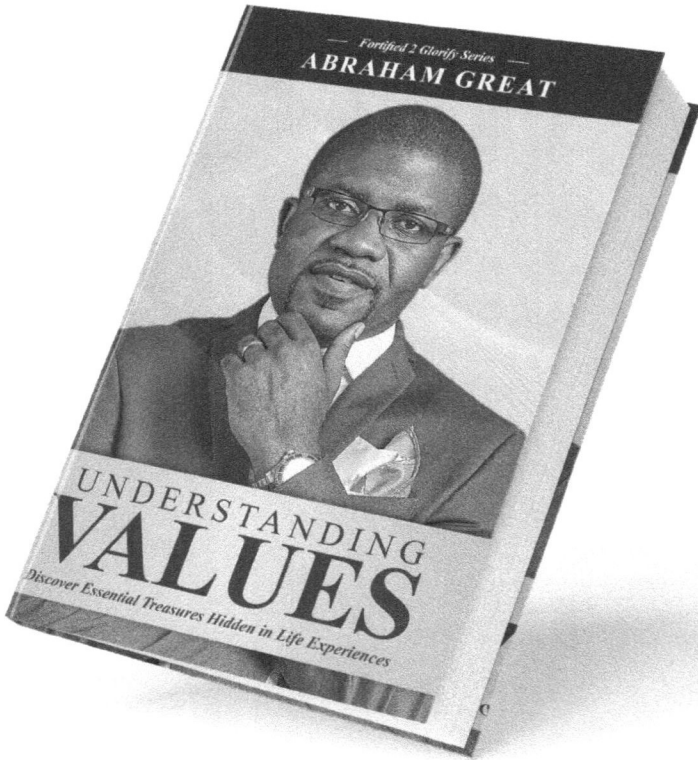

OTHER BOOKS BY
ABRAHAM GREAT

∎

Reconnecting Disconnected Generations

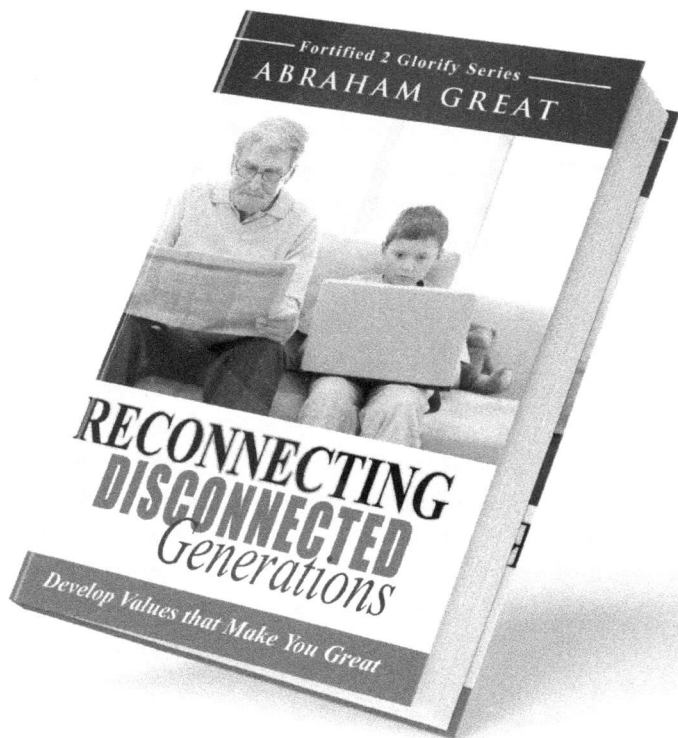

OTHER BOOKS BY
ABRAHAM GREAT

iThrive

www.ingramcontent.com/pod-product-compliance
Lightning Source LLC
Chambersburg PA
CBHW030311100426
42812CB00002B/655